Saying Goodbye
to Your Grief

Saying Goodbye to Your Grief

A book designed to help people
who have experienced crushing losses
survive and grow beyond the pain
into light of a new day

Hardy Clemons

Smyth & Helwys Publishing, Inc.®
Macon, Georgia

ISBN 1-880837-99-4

Saying Goodbye to Your Grief
by Hardy Clemons

Copyright © 1994
Smyth & Helwys Publishing, Inc.®
Macon, Georgia

Library of Congress Cataloging-in-Publication Data

Clemons, Hardy
    Saying goodbye to your grief: a book designed to
help people who have experienced crushing losses
survive and grow beyond the pain into light of a new
day / Hardy Clemons.
    viii + 86pp.   5" x 7" (12.8 x 17.8 cm.)
    Includes bibliographical references.
    ISBN 1-880837-99-4   (alk. paper)
    1. Grief—Religious aspects—Christianity. I. Title.
    BV4905.2.C55   1994
    248.8'6—dc20   94-13424
                                               CIP

Contents

To Ardelle
my friend and my wife

Foreword

Wayne E. Oates

Hardy Clemons is a veteran pastor who has written from pastoral experience this very easily-read volume on grief, one of the most common and universal experiences of life. Grief ranks up there right next to birth and death as an inescapable but inherent part of life.

This book is not a cumbersome textbook, nor is it a gushy, sentimental book about grief. No, it is packed full of stories, poems, scriptures, and specific guidance for a grieving person. The book is a handbook for the grieving person. It speaks in clear, basic English to every person's grieving heart and burdened life. It speaks of loss by death, but also loss in the fall of life—divorce, the losses in the normal process of growing up and older, job loss, etc.

If a pastor is a person of sorrows acquainted with grief he or she will find here resources with which to comfort those who mourn. More than that he or she will find comfort and wisdom for his or her own grief. Pastors are "not supposed" to "let on" that they are in grief, but the multiplicities of grief are there to bear, such as a congregation that insists on staying in constant conflict, or a pastor who is dismissed or "fired" by his or her congregation. Hardy Clemons' book is also a book for pastors ourselves.

This is not just a foreword to Hardy Clemons' book. I am a fellow sufferer with him in griefs he describes as his own. He speaks of the death of Grady Nutt, our mutual friend who died in a plane crash. He and I shared in that loss and comforted each other. The death of Laura Lue, John Claypool's daughter, we also shared together. We have been friends and confidants for four decades. He has comforted me in "losses in the face of life" such as changing jobs.

He speaks with specific stories that clarify each of his points. They are fresh, real, and moving stories. The book is an adventure in narrative theology. Especially is this true of the interpretation of Samuel's grief over Saul described in 1 Samuel 16 (48 ff). I commend this book to the broken-hearted and those who would comfort them. Family members can read it and find connection with each other, a common language of grief, which, as Tennyson says has "no language but a cry."

Wayne E. Oates
Louisville, Kentucky

Chapter 1

The Anatomy of Grief

Grief has brought agony to human beings since Adam and Eve lost the garden of Eden. Grief—one of the most excruciating traumas of life—has been here *forever*. Yet, humanity waited until the middle of the twentieth century before anyone wrote intentionally about the subject.

Since the mid-1940s, more specific help has been available. We still have much to learn about grief—and growing through and beyond it; but help is now more available—if and when we are willing to learn, grow, and work.

We dare not be glib in the face of grief—our own nor that of others. Grief is individual; no grief is exactly like another.

Grief is awful—particularly when it is your own. Lord Byron was right: He saw the reality of grief as the solitude of pain—the feeling that your heart is in pieces; your mind is a blank; "there's not a joy the world can give like that it takes away." [1]

Any loss causes grief. The more bereft one feels from the loss, the more agony the grief brings. To be devastating to one person, the loss does not have to seem painful or even significant to anyone else. Someone who does not understand your loss can easily say: "Get over it!" or some equivalent of "We'll get you another doggie." But, significant loss always causes significant pain.

Once during my first pastorate, my secretary phoned: "Shirley's second cousin has just died; she is devastated. She needs her pastor!" I went willingly, but I did not understand why this seemed so serious. On the way, I tried to think of what a second cousin really is, and if I knew any of mine.

When I arrived, I quickly learned that the "second cousin" was in fact the woman who—when "Shirley's" parents were killed in an auto accident when she was five years old—had taken her in, offered her a home, and been her mother all those years. She and Shirley had remained very close as Shirley grew into adulthood. The family records said "second cousin," but Shirley's heart said "Mommy!" Of course, I know now that the loss of her second mommy brought back to her conscious mind many of the agonies of the loss of her first mommy. Superficially, her loss sounded rather insignificant to a cub pastor. Actually, she was grieving a major loss and a double loss! We need to understand as much as possible about the anatomy of grief.

Eric Lindeman gave us a wonderful gift when he began his research following the tragic Coconut Grove fire in Boston in 1944. He approached the families who had lost loved ones in the fire and—with care, skill, and patient sensitivity—listened to their experiences. He kept careful notes then wrote his findings to help others struggling with loss. He documented what Wayne

Oates would phrase so well years later: "To go through grief, we must grow through grief." [2]

The world has been struggling with loss since Eden and the death of Abel, but not until 1944 did anyone document what tends to happen to humans when we experience loss. Not until 1970 did the first medical school in this country include a textbook on grief in its curriculum!

This latency may have been born of denial. We do not want to face our losses. My friend, Red Duke—surgeon at The University of Texas Health Sciences Center in Houston, the instigator of helicopter ambulances, and star of his own medical-help T.V. spot—said it well: "Denial is not a river in Egypt." Maybe we humans are so good at avoiding pain and the labor of grief that we really do not want to face the causes and remedies. Maybe we just trusted in folk cures too long. At any rate, we waited unnecessarily to have the knowledge now available about grief.

The heart of that knowledge is that any and all loss causes grief—the more serious the loss, the more painful the grief. I invite you to consider some of the many losses that comprise the anatomy of grief. I hope you will find help and encouragement for working with your own story of grief, as well as for listening to others in their stories. The great Miguel de Unamuno helped us learn that we heal from grief when we share our common griefs.

The Death of Someone
with Whom You Are Bonded

Death is not the only cause of grief, but it is probably the most prevalent and the first to come to mind. Of course, there are varying degrees of loss and varying degrees of grief surrounding loss through death.

Sudden, unexpected death is more difficult to grieve. When death slips into a nursing home in the still of night after a long debilitating illness, grief is still present. I learned when my mother died in 1983 after a long illness that death can be a terrific shock even when it is not a surprise. Sudden, surprising death offers a shock more toxic to our well-being, however. Numbness continues longer.

The death of someone with whom you are bonded is more severe than when someone is an aquaintance. Grief can surprise the care-givers because, as we have seen, relationships are not always what they seem.

How someone dies affects how we grieve. When we cannot or choose not to see the body, coming to grips with the reality of death can be more difficult and more prolonged. People fear "remembering the person as he or she is in the casket" unnecessarily. After the shock of death has abated, our memories usually cluster around active life and pleasant situations more than around pictures about death.

Violent death tends to occasion a more severe grief. If the body is mangled beyond recognition, or in cases of murder or suicide, grief seems to be harder to grow through.

The death of someone from whom we were estranged at the time or with whom we had positive or negative unfinished business, can be a harder grief to sustain.

Do not forget about animals. Some people have animals who are family members. Their deaths feel like the deaths of dear friends and are sometimes more difficult to grieve—particularly since those who are not animal lovers do not understand why grievers are not comforted by the suggestion that "we'll get you another doggie."

Divorce

Some people who have experienced both death and divorce report that divorce can be a harder grief to bear. Death has a final reality that divorce does not. Most divorces do not just occur. Most couples try repeatedly to "save the marriage." They separate and then reconcile. All the while, loss and grief multiplies. I heard the great Carl Whitaker, one of the gurus of family systems therapy, say categorically: "There is no such thing as divorce."

Divorce creates loss for everyone! The person who does not want the divorce may feel rejection. The person who wants it may feel failure. Children lose their parents. Grandparents lose their beloved. Friends have difficulty being friends with both of the couple. Everyone loses, but society does not respond as with death. Grief may go underground.

One of the most severe griefs with which I have dealt was that of a grandmother when her beloved grandson was divorced from her granddaughter-in-law, the apple of her eye. She loved her dearly. After a messy divorce, the grandmother was by default estranged in the evening of her own life from the "daughter she had always wanted" but never had. She groaned in agony and soon died. Grief can be terminal.

I know many adults who have never resolved the pain occasioned when their parents divorced. People have said to me for years: "We're going to wait 'til the children go to college before we divorce. We don't want to upset them." My experience is that adult children have as much difficulty with divorce as younger children—sometimes more! To have your home split just as you have launched from it into a new and insecure world can be ultimately traumatic.

Loss of a Job

My fifty-seven-year-old friend/deacon called me just after work: "I've been fired," he announced. He had been with the same company more than twenty years, but it had recently been acquired by a larger group. He was fifteen days short of having his retirement vested. "They called me in at 3:30 and told me to clean out my desk and turn in my keys. I don't know what I'm going to do! I don't know how I'll tell my family. At my age, I can't find another job. I've got two children still in college. I need to see my pastor."

Losing a job is usually more than loss of income. It involves loss of position, identity, opportunity, familiarity, and security-deeper-than-money. But few casseroles and cookies are delivered when divorce or job loss is the occasion for grief. Because my deacon friend understood the necessity of grief work, he grieved his loss in time and then went on to find another job that, in his words, "made me glad I got fired in the first place."

Moving Away from Your Place

My pastor-friend called for help: "I've seen this new woman in our church several times. She is sad, listless, and hard to communicate with. I can't help her. Would you see her?"

After a few minutes in my office, I saw what he meant. I probed and listened intently and incessantly, but could get nowhere. Finally I thought to ask: "Have you lost anything important to you recently?"

"Lost anything?" she almost roared. "Let me tell you what I've lost!"

A few months earlier her husband had called one afternoon to say, "I've got good news! I've been promoted, and my salary has almost been doubled. Oh, by the way, we will be moving to West Texas." Six months prior to that phone call, this couple had moved into their dream house. They had saved for it for years. It had been designed by an architect friend and constructed by a contractor the woman had known all her life. They had spared no expense and the result was beyond their fondest fantasy. The house was next door to "Judy's" dearest friend, with whom she had walked to kindergarten the first day and shared all the intimacies of growing up. They lived on a beautiful cul-de-sac in suburban Connecticut and had coffee together every morning. They were "best friends."

The day "Judy" and her husband arrived in our city —before airlines provided portable ramps from the plane and we had to brave the elements—the worst west Texas sandstorm anyone could remember blew all day. They moved into Holiday Inn, since there were "no adequate houses available to rent or buy." It would take nearly a year for an unknown builder to get their new house ready. West Texas seemed so brown and flat and dry. "There are no trees here," she kept saying.

Her husband was busy and occupied every day. He was excited about his new challenges, authority, and income level. She was lonely and angry but did not want to "rain on his parade." She said nothing to him or anyone of what she was feeling. She was depressed, felt betrayed, and was thinking of divorce.

"Have I lost anything?" she wailed. "I've lost everything but 'Henry,' and he never comes home anymore. And, when he does, he's too spent to relate to me. I'm dying!"

As "Judy" talked and I listened to her multiple losses, she began to come out of the shock and deprivation she felt. She began rebuilding her life in a strange place. She began talking to Henry about her loss and her feelings. Talking about the grief went so well that when Henry got another promotion several years later and could have returned to Connecticut with another whopping pay raise, she wanted to stay in Lubbock. And they did!

To paraphrase Wayne Oates—when we grow through grief we go through grief. Life can begin again after devastating loss. It can even be better.

Someone Leaving Home

When someone leaves home, grief usually happens. He or she may be going to military service (which is deepened with fear if the assignment is dangerous or life-threatening), to college, to get married, three blocks to first grade, or even to the barbershop for a son's first haircut (The hair that goes into that little envelope is not the major loss: "My last baby is growing up, and I can't stop crying.") The loss may hit when a daughter leaves in a car with a boy for her first date.

Some people leave home in anger. Some depart a disrupted family system. Siblings sometimes do not speak to each other for decades, or parents are cut off from children because of family secrets or unresolved grievances. This occasions a deeper, more anxiety-ridden grief. Guilt may lurk as a hidden monster in the basement of our minds and hearts.

Loss of Aim or Identity

"Joe" called me on Thanksgiving Day. "I apologize for calling today," he said, "but I've just got to see you while I'm home from school. My life has fallen apart!"

Joe was a young church member and at that time a freshman at a small college. I had noticed he had not been home all fall. Last year his name was a household word in our town. He was one of the most outstanding ball carriers our football fans had ever seen. When he walked the halls of his high school or the streets of the town, people punched each other and said, "Wow! There's Joe! He's great!" He was a celebrity.

Joe was too small to be of interest to the scouts of the major colleges and too proud to settle for a scholarship at one of the many smaller schools that sought him. He decided to attend a college where he knew no one and could "just be a student."

"It's just awful," he said when I asked him what he had lost. "No one knows me, no one cares. My life is over. I keep thinking of running my truck into a ditch. I'd come home and quit, but I'm embarrassed." He talked, and I listened and asked questions and listened some more. We met again whenever he was home. I called periodically on the phone.

By chance I talked to Joe a few weeks before writing this. He is now out of school, co-owner of a successful business, husband of a beautiful woman, and father of three bright children—one of whom is a "tiger" on the same high school gridiron. Now in mid-life, he told me of his gratitude for our pastoral conversations, and he spoke of his new aims and identity. "I can't believe I nearly ended it all and missed this," he said.

A Birth Defect, Surgery, or Illness

Birth defects, some kinds of surgery, chronic or debilitating illness, miscarriages, and many other medical ailments cause loss and, therefore, grief. My oldest cousin was born with Downs Syndrome. He was the first grandson on that side of the family and named for my grandfather. The family had great hopes for him. Even with his disability he was a beautiful person—warm, fun, real, loving! At the time of his death at age fifty-three, he could say three words: mama, kitty, and no. In our family system, we never talked about our pain. We tried to ignore it. All of us carried an unspoken grief we did not know how to manage. How I wish we had known how to speak our pain so as to receive the comfort and encouragement that was available.

Loss of a Dream or Opportunity

Many people grieve when they see time passing them by and realize they will never have the opportunity they sought and perhaps thought God had destined for them. My colleague in ministry commented years ago,

> I was never just right for the jobs I wanted. I would hear the bishop say, "You would be just right for that job if only you were a little older." Then, all of a sudden, he began to say, "You would really be right for that job if

only you were a little younger." I don't remember crossing the line!

One day the reality may dawn that you will never be head of the department, or manager, or dean, or president. Younger people are passing you by. Another version of this grief is that you **do** get to be CEO, or dean, or even President of the United States! Your dream comes true, your ship comes in, but you lack the power or prominence you envisioned, or the fulfillment is not as great as you imagined. Success feels barren.

Loss comes in many shapes and forms. With loss comes grief and the necessity of grief work, which is not unlike the labor of bearing a child. Failure, loss of face, embarrassment, losing your church or support group, loss of a relationship—so many losses occur as we journey through our pilgrimages.

In the movie, *Whose Life Is It Anyway?* Richard Dreyfuss played Ken Harrison, a brilliant young sculptor who survived a horrible auto accident that resulted in his being a quadriplegic. In an instant, he lost the dream of becoming one of the world's great sculptors. Furthermore, he lost the capacity to have any control over his life and destiny. He could not even refuse an unwanted injection from his doctor who wanted to sedate him, dull his pain, and calm his panic.

The professionals assigned to him did not seem to want to hear his despair about his losses. They tried to distract him, humor him, give him pep talks, entertain

him, and medicate him. No one ever asked the opera-
tive question: "Would you like to talk about your losses
and how you feel about them?" No one was willing to
listen!

I wish a script writer had written a skillful, caring
pastor—or even a Christian friend—into Ken Harrison's
life. If someone had invited him to talk about his losses
and feelings, just listening quietly; if someone in the
story had learned something about the anatomy of grief
and the gift of listening, Ken Harrison might have chosen to say goodbye to his grief and hello to a new life.

Notes

[1]Richard Ashley Rice, *The Best of Byron* (New York: Thomas
Nelson and Sons, 1942) 73.

[2]Wayne E. Oates, *Pastoral Care and Counseling in Grief and Separation* (Philadelphia: Fortress Press, 1976) 78.

Chapter 2

Stages in the Process of Grief

Grief seems such an endless pain. So many people are hurting; yet, they can move through grief. The wounds of grief can heal—though scars remain. Help, hope, peace, and new life are available *if* persons choose to suffer, work, and grow *through* a crushing loss instead of staying in it.

"Evelyn" and I were friends in college. We had not kept up with each other, so I was surprised to see her at a "widow's network" meeting where I spoke on dealing with grief. I learned that she had returned home one day and found her forty-year-old husband dead of a heart attack. When I asked how she was coping with such a sudden and tragic loss, she said in a thin, overly melodic voice: "Just fiiiine. I'm here to help the other people who aren't doing as well as I am." A little bell rang in my counselor's head: "I wonder how she's *really* doing?"

A few weeks later she called for an appointment. She had seen a doctor because of severe chest pains she was having. Her doctor had said: "Nothing is physically wrong with you, Evelyn. Your problem is that you haven't dealt with 'Sid's' death. Go see a counselor. Ask for help with the grief you still carry." Six years had passed since that tragic afternoon when she found "Sid" on the floor.

The first few times we met, Evelyn could not use the word "dead." When I used it, she visibly flinched.

She said, "I have a boulder the size of a large grapefruit in my chest. It won't go away. I don't want to go on living. I envy the nerve of my colleague who recently took her life."

To cut to the end of the story—after significant struggle and grief work, Evelyn was able to let go of her grief for Sid. Last January, I chanced to meet her in an airport on her way to a convention. She said,

> Thank you for helping me face and work through my grief. I have married a wonderful guy whose wife died two years ago. We are happy, I am happy, God is here, life is good. The boulder is gone!

If we are to deal creatively and redemptively with the grief that comes with any significant loss, we must make a painful choice to work through a developmental process. Although this process has been described in various ways by many counselors, I prefer the approach of Wayne Oates, distinguished professor at The Southern Baptist Theological Seminary and The University of Louisville School of Psychiatry. He is acknowledged as an international authority regarding grief work. He says people tend to work through six stages of grief.[1]

Shock

A major loss assaults us in such overpowering ways that we simply cannot accept it. We cannot quickly assimilate reality that is so unwelcome and so devastating. We may be stunned—as though we have had a physical blow to the head. We may be "in shock," or even act as though nothing serious has happened. We may seem "high" or even serene.

Numbness

When shock begins to subside, we may "freeze up" or feel little or nothing. Such numbness is God's way of helping us assimilate unwelcome facts as quickly as possible. During this period of grief, we may feel that family, friends, or even God are distant and do not care about us and our pain. Food may taste bland or "funny." We may not care about people or things that formerly mattered. We are tempted to withdraw excessively from people and activities and then misperceive that they have withdrawn from us.

Thomas made this mistake after Jesus' resurrection. He withdrew from the fellowship of the believers and went away to try and care for the wounds he sustained at Jesus' death. Having withdrawn into himself, away from the others, he missed the appearance of Jesus that John described (see John 20). We, too, may withdraw into ourselves and miss the resurrection God wants for us. Of course, some solitude is necessary in facing grief. At times, though, we must push ourselves to be with people, particularly the community of faith.

Alternating between Fantasy and Reality

At this stage of grief, we struggle continually between the reality of the unwelcome fact and the fantasy that "this is all a dream and the loss has not actually occurred." If we "steel ourselves" against the unwelcome reality, we usually experience an increase of destructive emotions. Anger, anxiety, guilt, depression, and/or cynicism may assault us so totally that we lose our ability to function normally, though we may not realize that we have done so. We may cling to or idolize our loss.

Some people remain in the fantasy phase and never recover. I know a woman in another state who still looks for the return of her son who died of cancer in 1959. When the phone rings, she thinks it is probably Mike. His baseball cap is still on the four-poster bed where he hung it before the last trip to the hospital. This woman is frozen in the fantasy phase of grief. She idolizes Mike and idealizes his life. She has withdrawn permanently into her myth that he is still alive. If she faced the reality side of grief, however, a breakthrough could occur that is painful but productive of new life.

Flooding of Emotions and Grief

At this stage, the wall between fantasy and reality breaks, and a flood of grief sweeps through and over us. We feel that "nothing will ever be right again; I will never recover from this agony." We may lose all meaning in our lives, become bitter, hostile, exceedingly weepy, or even feel "I am going crazy!"

Take heart! To grieve is not to be crazy. This flooding of emotions and grief is a necessary step in working *through* grief. When we face the flooding, we take the necessary step that leads to new life. The reverse of what we fear will happen actually happens. The fear says, "If I cry, I'll cry forever." The reality is, "If I don't let my tears come into the open, my crying will never cease."

One of my parishoners faced the loss of his marriage, the loss of his children, the loss of his job, and then cancer. He said after he had worked through his grief and re-established his life, "God gave me tears to wash away the pain."

Selective Memory and Stabbing Pain

After the out-pouring of flooding grief, the grief process usually levels off to a more drawn out and less intense day-to-day reassociation of memories. A sight, a smell, and/or a song may elicit memories that bring a briefer, stabbing pain.

Daytime fantasies and bereavement dreams relieve anxiety. Guilt, anger, loneliness, and other emotions continue. Light is seen at the end of a tunnel, however, reducing the feeling of being lost in a cave.

Acceptance of Loss / Reaffirmation of Life

When we reach this stage of grief, we have gone through a sort of death, burial, and resurrection regarding the loss. We experience a surprising reaffirmation of goals, values, and life itself. We are now capable of establishing new and meaningful relationships and re-entering old ones with new enthusiasm. When we accept, grieve, and relinquish loss, we can enjoy life again. The God who created us in the beginning and has walked with us "*through* the valley of shadows" can lead us into new life—even after a massive, crushing loss.

Remember, experiencing grief is somewhat like labor pains! Grief work demands almost more from us than we can muster. To refuse to do grief work, however, is to be stuck in the valley of the shadow of death. When we become willing to let go, our resurrection becomes possible. C. S. Lewis said it well: "Nothing that has not died will be resurrected."[2]

New life was possible for the Old Testament character Samuel in his grief about the self-destruction of King Saul (see 1 Sam 16). Samuel discovered the possibility for Israel to have a new king and a new beginning, and the new king turned out to be a greater king than Saul. But Samuel had to act! When he moved into action in response to God's command, he chose the new life God wanted him to have.

New life is a treasure God wants to help us discover during our grief. Grief can be a bridge to a deeper life with God as creator, redeemer, and sustainer. When I am bereft by the agony of grief, the God who lost His son wants to become my friend and companion in the journey of grief work.

Notes

[1]Wayne E. Oates, *Pastoral Care and Counseling in Grief and Separation.* (Philadelphia: Fortress Press, 1976) 79. See also Oates, *Anxiety in Christian Experience* (Philadelphia: Westminster Press) 51-56.

[2]C. S. Lewis, *The Weight of Glory*, cited in Rueben Job and Norman Shawchuck, *A Guide to Prayer for Ministers and Other Servants* (Nashville: The Upper Room) 185.

Chapter 3

Helping Each Other
Grieve Creatively

Troy Organ, distinguished professor emeritus of Philosophy at Ohio University in Athens, Ohio, experienced the death of his wife, Lorena, by suicide on 19 September 1978. Later, in an article for *The Christian Century*—"Grief and the Art of Consolation: A Personal Testimony"—he wrote:

> Consolation is indeed an art. It is the art of active love. Thanks to the consolation of those who listened, who touched, who invited me into their homes, who wept with me. I have found my way back to life. . . . I have received comfort from the Christian community, and I am indeed grateful to those who have sincerely tried to assist me in the very difficult task of dealing with the loss of a loved one through suicide. . . . As light displaces darkness, I recognize my debt to those who have been my comforters, and I pray that I have learned out of this experience both how to grieve and how to console.[1]

He informed my understanding of helping people in grief as much as anything I have ever read: "Grief is a helplessness that does not cry for help. One cries and hopes that help will come unbidden."[2]

So . . . I would like to make a few suggestions about relating helpfully to people who have had a major loss.

Go!

Be present! Maya Angelou said it well:

Lying, thinking
Last night
How to find my soul a home
Where water is not thirsty
And bread loaf is not stone.
I came up with one thing
And I don't believe I'm wrong
That nobody,
But nobody
Can make it out here alone.[3]

People say, "I want to go, but I don't know what to say." My response to that is, "Good. That's better! Say nothing. Just go, say 'I'm sorry, I care' and nothing else. Your presence will say everything that needs to be said." Most people say too much to grieving persons anyway.

If for some reason you cannot go,

Phone or Write!

Say: I'm sorry.
        I care.
            I love you.
            I'm here to help if I may.

It is not necessary or even important to say anything!

Listen!

Let the person in need of comfort talk! Let him or her talk about people . . . events . . . feelings. One of the major tasks of grief is for the loss to become real. Going and *listening* will aid this process.

Listen particularly for feelings. Accept these feelings without judgment! Feelings are not moral or immoral, good or bad—just feelings!

I have been there so many times as a pastor and have seen the scenario as people come to give the gift of their presence. I have heard the typical story:

> John has not been feeling well lately, but when he came in tonight he said he was feeling better. He ate such a good supper. His appetite seemed to be back. After supper he went in to listen to the news. I was puttering around the kitchen, finishing things. When I went in to join him, he seemed to be asleep in his chair. I tried not to disturb him, but then he seemed not to be moving at all. I spoke to him, then went over and touched him, and . . . he was gone!

Then, the phone or the door bell rings, and she tells the story all over again: "John hasn't been feeling well lately. But, tonight he came in and had such a good supper. Then, he went in to hear the news. . . ."

As caring people visit and call, she tells one of the most important stories of her life over and over again. Each time she repeats the story, the reality she is loathe to face sinks into her being a bit. For us to go and care and listen is so crucially important!

Ask Questions!

Brief questions, not nosy questions! Ask about feelings . . . events . . . people: "Would you be willing to . . . tell me about your daughter?" "What is it like for you to be divorced?"

Encourage the person to talk about the loss. Again, Troy Organ has observed:

> Friends poured in all afternoon. There were never less than a dozen people with me during the rest of the day. As each arrived, there was a brief expression of sorrow. Then conversation turned to the weather, politics, campus gossip. I wanted to talk about Lorena, but everyone else seemed to find this an embarrassing topic.[4]

Don't Preach!

Don't interpret! Don't explain! Don't give premature hope! Troy Organ said: "It's cruel to say grief will end."[5] Don't argue!

Touch!

Touch appropriately, of course, but do not lose the healing quality of compassionate human touch.

Offer Specific Help!

Don't say, "Call me if I can do anything." Instead, ask: "Could I pick anyone up at the airport for you?" "May I house some of the people coming from out of town?" "May I cut your lawn?" "May I pick you up for worship next Sunday? We'll get there right on time and leave as worship ends."

Troy Organ said the person who was the most help to him when his wife took her own life was the woman who said: "You are to be my guest every Thursday evening at 6:30 P.M. for supper. I have already set aside a napkin ring for you."[6]

People want to talk about their losses. They want us to listen to what they feel. We give them a priceless gift when we patiently listen to whatever they want to say. We neither judge nor argue nor tell them what to feel or how to face their loss. We listen.

My dear friends and fellow church members lost their teenage daughter and sister, Blair Smoak, in a tragic accident in 1992. In facing and seeking to work through their grief, they circulated an anonymous poem that invited people to speak with them about their darling Blair:

> The time of concern is over.
> No longer am I asked how my wife is doing.
> Too seldom is the name of our daughter mentioned to me.
> A curtain descends. The moment has passed.
> A life slips from frequent recall.
>
> There are exceptions: close and compassionate
>   friends,
> Sensitive and loving family, Blair's closest pals.
> For most, the drama is over.
> The spotlight is off. Applause is silent.
> But for me the play will never end.
> The effects on me are timeless.
> Say Blair to me.
>
> On the stage of my life she will always be
>   a rising star!
> Do not tiptoe around the most consuming event
>   of my life.
> Love does not die.
> Her name is written on my life. . . .
> Say Blair to me and say Blair again, and again.
>
> It hurts to bury her memory in silence—
>   and I will not. . . .
> So long as we are here, please
>   say Blair to us.[7]

Notes

[1]Troy Organ, "Grief and the Art of Consolation: A Personal Testimony," *The Christian Century* (1-8 August, 1979) 762.

[2] Ibid., 759

[3]Maya Angelou, *Poems* (New York: Bantam Books, 1986) 69.

[4]Organ, 760

[5]Ibid., 761.

[6]Ibid., 762.

[7]Anonymous, edited by Lewis and Betty Smoak.

Chapter 4

Saying Goodbye to Your Grief

Some people are not yet ready to say goodbye to grief. Others, much to their detriment, try to say goodbye to grief too quickly. Trying to get through grief too soon can be problematic. Refusing to say goodbye to grief when it is time to do so, however, can be disastrous. Many people never say goodbye to grief and thus never say hello to life again after some crushing loss.

I invite you to say goodbye to grief—at the appropriate time. God wants us to walk *through* the valley of the shadow of death—not just *in* the valley. Both the Old and New Testaments teach that we are invited by God to move beyond grief.

In Matthew 5:4, Jesus said the single most important thing that has ever been said about grief. Eugene Peterson paraphrases it:

> You're blessed when you feel you've lost what is most dear to you.
> Only then can you be embraced by the one most dear to you.[1]

Today's English Version translates this beatitude:

> Happy are those who mourn;
> God will comfort them!

I hear Jesus saying three things in this sentence. First, mourning is necessary. When we lose someone, we must grieve! Second, we are blessed when we choose to mourn instead of avoiding pain. Trying to avoid pain is always unsuccesful and increases the pain we seek to dodge. Third, when we grieve our losses, we can ultimately say goodbye to grief, and we experience that state of well-being that the Bible calls blessed.

1 Samuel 15:34–16:1 tells a story that provides important clues to how we may choose to deal with our grief:

> Then Samuel went to Ramah, and Saul went up to his house in Gibeah, and Samuel did not see Saul again until the day of his death. But Samuel grieved continuously over Saul and the Lord repented that he had made Saul king over Israel. So the Lord said to Samuel, "How long will you keep on grieving over Saul, seeing that I have rejected him from being king over Israel? Fill your horn with oil and go, and I will send you to Jesse, the Bethlehemite, for I have provided for myself among his sons, a king for the country."

In these few verses of scripture, we are offered three basic insights into the phenomenon that we call grief. First, grief is blessed by God as a necessary reality when significant loss has occurred. It is natural, normal, and productive. God did not criticize Samuel for his grief over Saul. Second, grief is occasioned by losses other than death. Any significant loss will occasion the need for grief. Finally, at some point, God invites us, as he did Samuel, to say goodbye to grief and move on with the joy and responsibilities of living. God knows we cannot move on with life until we have finished our grief work.

To try to take grief away from people is not wise. When the time is appropriate to let grief go, it is necessary to do so. To turn grief over to God is to experience resurrection from grief, just as Jesus experienced resurrection from death—but only after he faced death!

Several years ago, I heard Fred Craddock talk about an experience at the time of his mother's death. (Craddock is one of the most competent interpreters of scripture in our world today. He taught New Testament interpretation and preaching at Candler School of Theology in Atlanta and is now retired.) Craddock said that following his mother's death, a woman entered his home on the afternoon prior to the funeral, carrying a very large Bible. The woman emoted,

> Isn't it great that your mother is now with the Lord? Isn't it wonderful that your mother is no longer here? She has been released from her suffering. You should all be so grateful!

She was saying the kind of thing that all of us have felt after someone's long illness. When we have made such statements, we have been well-motivated and well-intentioned in trying to help. This lady, as sometimes people are prone to do, was overstating her point, however.

Finally, Craddock said, "I couldn't take it any more. I got up and addressed this woman, and said:"

> Madam, I know that you mean well, and I know you do not intend to create a problem with us here by what you are saying. However, if you will read that Bible you are carrying around, you will notice that it does not simply say, "He is risen." It says, "*He is not here. He is risen.*" The same thing is true of our mother. We know that our mother is in a better place. We know that our mother is free of her suffering. But, please don't try to take our grief away from us. Please don't make us feel guilty about our pain. The truth is, we miss our mother.[2]

This episode capsulizes the two sides of the reality we must deal with if we are going to say goodbye to grief. Jesus did not get to the resurrection without going through the cross, and neither will we. If we are to become able to participate in the renewal of life that is offered in the reality of the resurrection of Jesus Christ, we must experience our own garden of Gethsemane. Hope lies on both sides—in the cross and in the resurrection. Jesus got to the resurrection by going through the cross, the death, the burial, the tomb—the tears, the agony, the loneliness, the anger, the frustration, and the devastation.

New life does not just happen. Freedom from grief does not just occur. Wayne Oates said it well: "We don't just *go* through grief, we *grow* through it."[3]

Failure to grow in the process of grief causes some people to never really re-establish their lives following a gigantic grief. They are unwilling to experience the pain and the darkness of the tomb.

I suggest four actions to help you say goodbye to grief—to grow through grief so that you may move beyond it and be restored by God to the newness of life God wants you to have.

Say Hello to Grief Work

First, to say goodbye to grief, begin by saying hello to grief work. The theorists who explain the process of grief with a major loss have chosen the word "work" to talk about the reality of grief. They speak of "grief-WORK."

You can never say goodbye to grief that you have not owned and internalized. It must be *your* grief. It must be allowed to surface. You must be allowed—by others and by yourself—to grieve, to mourn, to face and feel the pain.

First, to say hello to grief work, accept the pain of the loss. You cannot experience grief work without experiencing pain. Our culture teaches avoidance and denial of pain from the loss of something or someone that is deeply valuable. Non-acceptance of that pain means the lack of grief work. Avoidance of that pain means denial and delay of the grief work and resurrection that follows it.

Second, allow and accept the comfort that people offer, even though it is so easy to deny that we have any pain.

My mother died in 1983. People came from the most surprising places to offer comfort. They came to me by letter and telephone and in person to say, "I am sorry about your mother. She was an important person to me. I want you to know that I share your sorrow at her death."

Everything in me wanted to explain away my pain in losing my mother: "She was past eighty years old. She had been ill for quite a long time. She had a long, productive life. She was ready to go, and really it is a good thing that she could. Her death was a release for her, for my father, and for me."

Of course, all of that was true. But, if I focused on that release too soon and dodged the reality that it was painful to lose someone I loved, then I would have missed the grief work, as well as the resurrection that could occur at the other side of grief.

Third, to say hello to grief work, keep reviewing the loss. Remember, rehearse, talk about, and feel feelings —both positive and negative—about the loss.

Fourth, accept the many fears that come with grief: "Who else am I going to lose? What else is going to happen? Bad things happen in threes." (I have never been able to find that verse in the Bible, but many people are convinced that it is true.) Insanity, being overwhelmed, hostility carrying you away, "if I ever start crying I will never be able to stop"—these fears must be accepted and expressed.

Fifth, exercise the freedom to express sorrow, the sense of loss, guilt, anger, or agony. Allow the grief to surface; do not keep it hidden inside your personality. Pour out your feelings as a part of the grief work.

Sixth, be aware that you are constantly moving in a struggle between the various stages of grief until a reaffirmation of life is given by God. The stages of grief do not occur in a simple or well-structured manner, so do not just go through them, grow through them.

Finally, say goodbye to *your* grief—not grief in general or pain in general. Say goodbye to grief that you have owned and internalized. Feel the pain—your own pain, your own loss, your own agony of mourning.

Say Goodbye to Your Loss

To say goodbye to grief, say goodbye to loss.

Grady Nutt, the great humorist and T.V. star, was my good friend from our teenage years. Several years ago he called me and said, "I want to tell you a great story." Grady was one of the greatest storytellers I have ever known. He called frequently with a funny story, so I fastened my seat belt for one. This story was not funny, however. It was profound. I am so glad I heard it before I had to face Grady's death—and my own grief about his death.

He said,

> I was talking to a pastor friend of mine who was talking to a funeral director friend of his in Texas yesterday. For years he has been one of the most effective funeral directors in the Dallas area.
>
> Recently he learned that he had terminal cancer and only had a short period of time to live. This courageous man called his whole family together in the den of his home and sat them down. "I want to tell you something," he said. "I have learned that I have terminal cancer. I do not have long to live. I have watched people from the vantage point of the funeral profession all my life. I have helped people bury their dead for decades, and I want to tell the people who are dearest to me in all the world something extremely important. Listen to me carefully:
>
> > When I die, bury me.
> > If you won't let me die,
> > I will never let you live."[4]

I wrote the advice down and memorized it. (Grady, not knowing that he was less than a month away from his own death, gathered his family together and told them this story.) The advice is not easy to take, but to say goodbye to grief, you must relinquish your loss—turn loose the person that you loved.

I had that experience when Grady died. Seldom in my lifetime have I been so assaulted by a loss and so devastated by a grief such as that I experienced when he died. I answered the phone at 2:18 A.M. and heard another good friend say, "I have bad news. Grady is dead."

"Dead?!"

"Killed in an airplane crash!"

I thought: "There is some mistake—that cannot be. I was with him in San Antonio last week." I went through all that we go through when a death occurs. I was in agony immediately and continuously. I was in denial and shock. I could not believe it!

After a while, I had a dream. I was on a very high tower that seemed to be more than the height of the highest airplane from which I have ever looked out. I could look down and see the earth beneath me. It seemed about 80,000 feet below. The platform on this tower was about the size of a boxing ring. It had a very thin, rickety picket fence around it.

While I was standing and looking from this platform I thought: "Man, if I fell off this thing, I would fall forever. This is not a safe place to be. I need to get down."

Suddenly, Grady appeared! He was bopping around, dancing like Snoopy does in the comics and on television—just dancing around, celebrating life, and having a wonderful time. I was thinking, "That crazy guy needs to be careful or he is going to fall off this thing."

About that time he spun around, backed into that little picket fence, and fell through it. I rushed over to the side and watched for what seemed an eternity in my dream. He fell and fell and fell and fell. There is no way I can describe to you the agony I felt in the dream as he fell.

After what seemed an eternity, I saw two clouds shaped like strong, muscular arms reach out and catch Grady. Then, these giant arms enfolded him into a big hug. I woke up. I felt a sense of peace.

On one hand, the pain was still there; on the other hand, I had let go of the person I had lost. I had the most profound feeling that it was God whose arms I saw. I learned again that if I am ever going to say goodbye to grief, I have to relinquish the loss. I have to accept the reality that the person is gone and will not be back.

To say goodbye to grief, accept the loss, and relinquish the person or thing you have lost.

Say Hello to God

A third step seems to be foundational: saying hello to God. First, I invited you to say hello to grief work. Then, I invited you to say goodbye to your loss. Now, I am inviting you to say hello to God.

Many people would be critical of hearing a minister say as much as I have said without mentioning the necessity of turning to God with your grief. I have had enough experience with my own grief and that of other people to know that unless you are ready to say hello to God, it is too early to try to do so.

At some point, the grief sufferer likely will be able to affirm with the great psalmist, "When I walk through the valley of the shadow of death, I will fear no evil for thou art with me." We will be able to quit talking about God and start talking to God: "Thou art with me." But it may take a while to be ready to let God have your grief.

I have learned that when I can say hello to God, it helps me to say goodbye to my grief. I cannot say hello to God until I have done some grief work, however, or the effort will be abortive.

Wayne Oates has said, "The asunderness of life is not healed by nostalgia."[5] I would add not by time, keeping busy, or any of the other bromides that our culture recommends. Oates continues: "The asunderness of life is healed by translating our terror of the future into reverence for God."[6] To say goodbye to grief, you must say hello to the God who wants resurrection to happen again—this time in your life.

Saying hello to God is what I believe my dream helped me do following the death of my friend Grady.

Say Hello to Your Future

Finally, to say goodbye to grief, say hello to your future as God's gift of resurrected life, after you say hello to God in your grief. God gives the gift of resurrection and enables you to say hello to the future.

This hope for saying hello to God can be offered too early, too strongly, or too glibly. But, it is hope that the resurrection that occurred following the loss of God's only begotten son is a resurrection that is capable of happening again following whatever loss you grieve.

Harvey Cox, the Harvard theologian, once said: "In grief we are caught between nostalgia on one hand and fear of the future on the other. Fearing the future, we shrink back into nostalgia."[7]

I remind you that Oates said, "The asunderness of life is healed, not by nostalgia, but by translating our terror of the future into reverence for God and faith in God."

My colleague, John Claypool, and I shared the death of Grady Nutt. He and I were serving on the pastoral team of Second Baptist Church in Lubbock, Texas, when Grady was killed. John had been Grady's pastor in Louisville, Kentucky. Grady had been with us for a four-day emphasis in our congregation in Lubbock three weeks before his death. As we struggled with the tragedy of Grady's death, John told me of an experience he had at Laity Lodge shortly before going to Lubbock.

John's eight-and-a-half-year-old daughter, Laura Lue, had been diagnosed with acute leukemia. Eighteen months and ten days later she died. One night about twelve years later, when Laura Lue would have been twenty-three, John spoke at Laity Lodge in the wilds of southwest Texas. The next morning he went to breakfast. A lady he had not met the evening before came up to him and said, "Dr. Claypool, I need to talk with you." He could tell from the look in her eyes that she was deeply serious. She said, "I had an experience last night that I do not know what to do about, but I feel I must share it with you, though I am hesitant to do so."

He said, "Please go ahead. I am eager to help if I may," not knowing what she would say. She told this story:

"I had a dream last night. I dreamed that I was in England, at Oxford University, in the library. I was walking through the library trying to be quiet, trying not to disturb anyone, when I saw a beautiful blonde-haired woman in her early twenties sitting at a desk in the library. As I looked at her, I thought, 'What a beautiful young woman she is. I wonder what she is preparing herself for?' "

She motioned to me, and I went over to her. The young woman said to me in my dream, "My name is Dr. Claypool, and I understand that you know my father."

I said, "That is not exactly true, I really don't know your father. I have heard him speak and I know of him, but we are not friends, even acquaintances."

The young woman rushed right past that and said, "I wonder if you would be willing to take my father a message?"

I said, "Yes, I suppose I would."

She said, "Tell my father that I am here at Oxford working in leukemia research, and I am right on the edge of a breakthrough that will help people be able to recover from this dreaded, terminal illness. We get right to the edge of being able to make the discovery we are so eager to make, and then it falls apart in our hands. We have to back off, regroup, and begin again. We get there and we lose it, and we get there and we lose it. I have become convinced that the reason we cannot make this breakthrough is that my father won't let me go. Would you please, the next time you see my father, ask him to turn me loose? Ask him: 'Will you please let me go on with my life and you go on with yours?' "

John said, "It helped. It helped me to do what I had been trying without success to do since the day of her death. The woman's dream was a gift of God to me that allowed me to let Laura Lue go."[8]

Brian Wren's resurrection hymn helps me hear a word from God:

When grief is raw and music goes unheard,
    and thought is numb,
We have no polished phrases to recite.
You are our Lord, in faith we grasp familiar words:
    "I am the resurrection. I am life."

When time gives room for gratitude and tears,
Lord, make us free to grieve, remember, honor,
    and delight.
Let love be strong to bear regrets and banish fears.
    "I am the resurrection. I am life."

The height and breadth of what your love prepares
Soar out of time beyond our speculation and our sight.
The cross remains to earth the promise that it bears.
    "I am the resurrection. I am life."

All shall be judged, the greatest and the least,
    and all be loved,
Till every heart is healed, all wrong set right.
Sing and be glad, the Lamb prepares his wedding feast,
    And in the midst of death, we are in life.[9]

It is possible to say goodbye to even *your* grief. It is possible that the same divine energy that raised Jesus Christ from death can raise you to new life. If you are ready to say goodbye to your grief, if you need to say hello to your future, I pray that you will choose to do so. Say goodbye to your grief and hello to your future.

I invite you: Say hello to grief work. Say goodbye to your loss. Say hello to God. Say hello to your future. As you do, you will say goodbye to your grief. May I wish you "good journey" as you seek to do so.

Notes

[1]Eugene Peterson, *The Message* (Colorado Springs Co: NavPress, 1993) 15-16.

[2]Sermon at Alamo Heights United Methodist Church, San Antonio, Texas.

[3]Wayne E. Oates, *Pastoral Care and Counseling in Grief and Separation* (Philadelphia: Fortress Press, 1976) 79.

[4]Telephone conversation with Grady Nutt, October, 1982.

[5]Oates, Ibid.

[6]Ibid., 78.

[7]Ibid., 79.

[8]With permission of John Claypool

[9]Brian Wren, *Faith Looking Forward* (Carol Stream IL: Hope Publishing, 1983) 32

Chapter 5

How Long Does
It Take to Grieve?

I grew up thinking that real Christians do not grieve. I thought if one believed in God, he or she was insulated against grief and the pain of loss. When I started reading the Bible and the literature of grief, I realized that we all grieve when we lose something or someone valuable. The difference in Christians and others is, to quote Paul the apostle, that Christians do not grieve "as those who have no hope" (1 Thess 4:13, TEV).

Christians work through their grief with the companionship of Jesus the Christ who suffered and died. Christians are given the encouragement and strength of God who lost His only son. God as Father, Son, and Spirit shares our griefs and helps us work through and beyond our sorrows. As Brian Wren's great hymn invites us to sing:

> If faith comes true and Jesus lives,
> There'll be an end to grieving![1]

How long does it take to come to the end of grieving? People ask me frequently, "Pastor, how long will this awful grief last?" I mentioned earlier my friend "Evelyn" who, six years after her husband's untimely death, could still not utter the word "dead." She said again and again as we mourned her loss, "This agony will never end. This grapefruit-sized stone in my chest will never go away. My life is over!" Yet, through redemptive grief work, she learned that her life was not over. In the power of God, it began again—to the point that she expressed true joy to me.

How long does it take to grieve?

In one sense, grief lasts forever. We must face the fact that when major loss occurs, we will always remember the person or the "something" that was lost, and when we remember painful loss, we feel pain.

In another sense, grief does end, and new life begins. This new life occurs on the other side of grief work when we have walked "*through* the valley of the shadow of death."

Samuel learned about the end of grief and new life from Yahweh at Ramah. Samuel learned that God wants a statute of limitations on our grief so that, at some point, we may go on with our lives in the recovery of strength and joy—even though we continue to remember our loss. God did not criticize Samuel for grieving. Rather, he invited Samuel to lay aside his grief and move on into the exciting and valid discovery of a new king for Israel:

> How long will you go on grieving over Saul? I have rejected him from being king over Israel. Now, get some olive oil and go to Bethlehem to a man named Jesse. I have chosen one of his sons to be king. (1 Sam 16:1, TEV)

I hear God saying to Samuel: "Get your ordaining kit and go! You have grieved long enough. It's time to go on with your life." God was inviting Samuel to move beyond the threatening events of King Saul's demise into a new level of security and well-being in the development of God's new plan for Israel. We can learn from this if we will.

It was not that Samuel did not have a genuine loss to grieve or that God was unsympathetic with his taking a while to grieve. Saul had been a great king. He was tall, mighty, and powerful. He won victories and established control. And, he was religious! He believed the right "believables." He sacrificed correctly in the religious observances. His attitiude and behavior were the problems. He was disobedient to Yahweh, so God rejected him as king (see 1 Sam 15:22-23).

Samuel grieved this loss in agony. "As long as he lived he never again saw the king; but he grieved over him" (1 Sam 15:34, TEV). Samuel felt betrayed. What he had devoted his life to was coming apart. He was angry, discouraged, empty, and in pain. Saul had led the people away from God in the name of doing the work of God. Samuel was disappointed and at his wit's end. He grieved mightily over what Saul had done to himself and the people of Israel. God was sympathetic to Samuel. God was grieving, too, but God was more invested in renewal than loss. God focused on moving on with life into the creativity and joy of a new day.

God wanted to help Samuel grow through and beyond his grief.

Monica McGoldrick has helped me with my griefs and attempts to invite others to grieve and then move on. She has written:

> The primary goal of therapeutic intervention around death (or any other loss) is to empower and strengthen families to mourn their losses and move on.[2]

McGoldrick suggests four answers to the question: How long will it take to grieve this loss? She says it takes long enough to:

(1) Share the acknowledgement of the reality of the loss.
(2) Share the experience of the loss and put it into context.
(3) Reorganize your family or personal system and make the necessary shifts in critical roles.
(4) Reinvest in other relationships and life pursuits.

As noted in chapter two, Wayne Oates suggests that it takes long enough to work through the levels of shock, numbness, alternating between fantasy that the loss has not occurred and the reality that it has, the flooding of thought and emotions, selective memory and stabbing pain, and, finally, the acceptance of the loss and the reestablishment of life.[3]

Both McGoldrick and Oates offer hope that grief will end and new life will begin. Steps one and two in Oates' construct are similar to step one in McGoldrick's.

Through shock and numbness we struggle to acknowledge the reality of loss. The alternating and flooding stages of Oates correspond to McGoldrick calling for sharing the experience of the loss and putting it into context.

The play and movie *Steel Magnolias* has a touching example of how differently some people deal with the same loss. In the story, M'Lynn is the mother (played by Sally Fields) of a beautiful daughter, Shelby (played by Julia Roberts), who is diabetic and needs a kidney transplant. M'Lynn decides to donate the necessary kidney, but Shelby's body rejects the kidney. She is put on life support systems. After an agonizing period of time, the family decides that the merciful choice is to unplug the respirator that is prolonging Shelby's death but not her life. After the graveside worship, M'Lynn continues her grief work with her network of female friends—the "Steel Magnolias." She says something like:

> They turned off the machines. Drum (her husband) left. He couldn't take it. Jackson (Shelby's husband) left. It's sort of amusing in a way. Men are supposed to be made of steel or something.
>
> I just sat there. I held Shelby's hand. There was no noise, no tremble. Just peace.
>
> O God! I realize how *lucky* I am! I was there when that wonderful creature drifted into my life, and I was there when she drifted out.
>
> It was the most precious moment of my life.[4]

This powerful scene in the movie is an example of how the mother and the women in her network of friends struggle to put such an unwelcome death into the larger context of the cycle of life. M'Lynn's sense of privilege and giftedness at being there when Shelby's life began and when it ended, as agonizing as it was for her, gives meaning to her life and pain. Even as she leaves the graveside in abject agony about the loss of her daughter, she is already focusing on the total context of gift and not just the agony of her loss or that final experience.

The viewer is left with the notion that M'Lynn and these other "Steel Magnolias" are going to rise to the occasion, reorganize the expanded family system, and move on with life—even amid such excruciating loss and pain.

The movie helped me focus on what Samuel learned in visiting Jesse's household: Grief begins to end when one accepts the loss, focuses on God who gives the gift of life, and then moves on into the realization that resurrection of meaning and joy *do* follow the laborious work of grief.

In an earlier scene of *Steel Magnolias*, Shelby had given articulate testimony to the quality she wanted in her life and the way she felt about risking death to have a child. Her mother was trying to convince her to take the cautious path and not have children, so as not to take so much risk with her already frail body. Shelby

wanted her mother to see that how long her life lasted
was not as important to her as how fully she lived. She
said:

> Momma, I'd rather have thirty minutes of wonderful than
> a whole lifetime of nothin' special.

The closing scene in *Steel Magnolias* furnishes an ex-
cellent framework for getting grief work started. We see
tears, anger, tenderness, concern, unreadiness to be religious, laughter, gallows humor—all the stuff of which
grief and grief work are made. We see the importance
of friends being with each other as loss happens and
grief work begins. This is one of the most poignant
scenes in literature concerning how grief expresses itself
in such cataclysmic changes of emotional direction.

After the funeral is over and the crowd has left the
graveside, M'Lynn is standing at the casket alone. One
of her friends approaches:

Friend: "How you holdin' up honey?"

M'Lynn: "Fine."

Friend: "It was a beautiful service. The flowers were
the most beautiful I have ever seen."

M'Lynn: "They were beautiful."

Then, Annelle, the immature religious stereotype of
the movie speaks: "Miss M'Lynn, it should make you
feel better that Shelby is with her king."

M'Lynn: "Yes, Annelle, I guess it should."

Annelle: "We should all be rejoicing!"

M'Lynn: (irritated) "You go on ahead. I'm sorry if I don't feel like it. I guess I'm a little selfish. I'd rather have her here."

Annelle: "Miss M'Lynn, I don't mean to upset you by sayin' that. It's just that when something like this happens, I pray very hard to make heads or tails of it. And, I think that in Shelby's case, she just wanted to take care of that little baby and of you, and of everybody she knew. And her poor little body was just worn out. It just wouldn't let her do all the things she wanted to—so she went on to a place where she could be a guardian angel. She will always be young. She will always be beautiful. And, I personally feel much safer knowing that she is up there on my side. It may sound real simple and stupid, and maybe I am—but, that's how I get through things like this."

M'Lynn: "I 'preciate that. And it's a real good idea. Shelby, as you know, wouldn't want us to get mired down and wallow in all this. She would want us to handle it the best way we know how and get on with it. That's what my mind says. I just wish somebody'd explain it to my heart!" (Tears.)

Another of the friends: "O honey are you ok?"

M'Lynn: "I'm fine. I'm *fine*!! I can jog all the way to Texas and back, and my daughter never could. I'm so *mad* I don't know what to do. I want to know why! I want to know why Shelby's life is over. I want to know how that baby will ever know how wonderful his mother was, what she went through for him. No. No!! No!!! *No*!!!! It's not supposed to happen this way! I'm supposed to go first! I've always been ready to go first. I don't think I can take this! I don't think I can *take* this! I just want to hit somebody 'til they feel as bad as I do. I just want to hit something. I want to hit it *hard*!"

One of the friends: "Here! Hit this." The friend grabs Ouisa, the stereotypical heavyweight of the movie, and pulls her into place for M'Lynn to hit. "Go ahead, M'Lynn. Hit her hard. We'll make a T-shirt: 'I slapped Ouisa Boudreaux.' Hit her! Ouisa! This is your chance to do something for your fellowman. M'Lynn, knock her lights out."

Friend: "M'Lynn, you just missed the chance of a lifetime. Everyone in Chickapin parish would give their eye teeth to take a whack at Ouisa!"

Ouisa responds to the friend, "You are a pig from hell."

The agony, the anger, the questions, the religious speeches, the urge to hurt someone, the gallows humor all illustrate the kaleidoscope of feelings that assault us when we lose someone or something we love dearly.

The scene in the movie points to the necessity of letting our feelings—whatever they are—express themselves. Such expression of feelings begins the grief process and moves us in a direction of healing and wholeness. If such feelings are denied or bottled up, they go underground and find expression in less healthy, destructive ways. Grief work can never be completed until it begins.

Grief work can never begin until we are willing to start at an unskilled, uncomfortable level. We must get started, even though we feel foolish in the process, even though we feel uncertain about how to proceed.

Everything I was taught as a child about expressing and not expressing feelings gets in my way when I must grieve. Everything in me says: "Big boys don't cry! Nice boys don't get mad! If you can't say something positive, don't say anything at all. Real athletes play hurt and ignore their pain."

While these thoughts may have some valid place in our lives, they do not apply to grief and the labor of grief. I have learned that to do something skillfully and appropriately I have to do it first unskillfully and uncomfortably. I have learned that the ancient cultures that wore black armbands and observed periods of mourning and recovery after massive loss had a wisdom we would do well to emulate. If I do not face my grief and work through it and grow through it, I will grieve longer than necessary and never go on with my life. If I won't let my loss die, it will indeed not let me live. If I stay in love with my loss or my grief, my love becomes a sarcophagus. If I mourn my loss, embrace my pain, and follow the one who is "a man of sorrows, acquainted with grief," life can become whole and new again.

M'Lynn was right. "We've just got to do the best we can."

So, how long does it take to grieve?

(1) Long enough to focus on the gift rather than the loss,

(2) Long enough to face the loss and put it into context with the rest of your life,

(3) Long enough to follow the leadership of God into the discovery of new life—which may in some ways be even better than the old one,

(4) Long enough to respond to new challenges of sharing grace with others in the agonies of their grief.

Grief begins to end when we can focus on the gift. While the loss never ebbs completely, the gift can transcend the loss and furnish a new impetus to accept the challenge of going on with life. It is not easy to focus on the gift, but it can happen.

John Claypool told an instructive story at the conclusion of his sermon "Life is Gift," following the death of his daughter, Laura Lue. While he was growing up, John's family had no washing machine. When an associate of John's father was drafted in World War II, he suggested that the Claypools use his washing machine while he was away. John said: "So this is what we did, and it helped us a great deal."[5] He added:

> But eventually the war ended, and our friends returned; in the meantime I had forgotten how the machine had come to be in our basement in the first place. When

they came and took it, I was terribly upset, and I said so quite openly.

My mother, being the wise woman she is, sat me down and put things in perspective for me: "Wait a minute, son. You must remember, that machine never belonged to us in the first place. That we ever got to use it at all was a gift. So, instead of being mad at its being taken away, let's use this occasion to be grateful that we had it at all."[6]

Then, Claypool added his own salient wisdom concerning Laura Lue's death—even amid the pain and agony of her tragic loss:

Here, in a nutshell, is what it means to understand something as a gift and to handle it with gratitude, a perspective biblical religion puts around all of life. And I am here to testify that this is the only way down from the mountain of loss. I do not mean to say that such a perspective makes things easy, for it does not. But, at least it makes things bearable when I remember that Laura Lue was a gift, pure and simple, something I neither earned nor deserved nor had a right to. And when I remember that the appropriate response to a gift, even when it is taken away, is gratitude, then I am better able to try and thank God that I was ever given her in the first place.[7]

He then invited his congregation: "Will you join me in trying to learn to travel this way?"[8]

I know that my friend, John, still feels pain about his beloved Laura Lue and always will. I also know that he travels the roadway of gratitude as his avenue of life. He has become a wounded healer to many others and to me. He has been a steward of his suffering and wisdom. He has used "the clay of his suffering to make a healing balm"[9] and shared it with us in our agony.

When my wife, Ardelle, struggled with what we thought could be a terminal malignancy in 1976, when Grady Nutt's death devastated me in 1982, when my mother's death left me in shock (though not surprise) in 1983, John was more than my colleague and partner in ministry. He was more than my friend. He was my minister and teacher concerning the life that is a gift of God.

He helped me say hello to grief work, goodbye to my losses, and hello to God and God's gracious gifts. Most of all, he helped me focus on life as a precious, priceless gift from God. He helped me to focus on what I had been given more than on what I had lost. In doing so, thank God, John helped me say hello to my future.

How long does it take to grieve? Long enough to focus on the gift more than the loss. Long enough to trust the God who is giver of all gifts with the well being of your self and your future. Long enough to decide to go on with the priceless gift of life—grateful for what you lost, hopeful in your new beginning!

Notes

[1]Brian Wren, *Faith Looking Forward* (Carol Stream IL: Hope Publishing Co., 1983) 31.

[2]Monica McGoldrick, "Echoes from the Past: Helping Families Mourn Their Losses," in *Living Beyond Loss: Death in the Family*, eds. Monica McGoldrick and Froma Walsh (New York: W. W. Norton and Co., 1991) 54-55.

[3]Wayne E. Oates, *Anxiety in Religious Experience* (Philadelphia: Westminster Press) 51-56.

[4]*Steel Magnolias*, prod. Ray Stark and dir. Herbert Ross, 118 min., Tri-Star Pictures, 1990, videocassette.

[5]John Claypool, *Tracks of a Fellow Struggler* (Waco: Word, Inc., 1974) 81.

[6]Ibid.

[7]Ibid., 81-82.

[8]Ibid., 82-83.

[9]Carlyle Marney, *These Things Remain* (Nashville: Abingdon-Cokesbury, 1953) 60.

Chapter 6

Lightposts on
the Journey to New life

Introduction

I am most hesitant—in fact, unwilling—to "tamper" with scripture. I am not a professional translator of Hebrew or Greek, and I believe we must take the Bible very seriously.

Yet, as a pastor and pastoral psychotherapist, I have found that putting the scripture in the language people use on a daily basis furnishes them with fresh biblical and spiritual insights that even my limited proficiency with translating and paraphrasing scripture can offer. As I have struggled with how to be helpful to my own congregation, it has occurred to me that paraphrases such as the ones I have included here—read from a grieving person's viewpoint—speak profound truth.

When someone is finding it very difficult to turn loose of grief, God can speak through the Bible and help with the painful process of letting that grief go.

I invite you to look and listen for a word from God in these passages. Read them silently. Read then aloud to yourself. Read them to someone else. Listen! Listen for a word from God!

Hebrews 12:12–29
A paraphrase with reference to grief work

I know, my beloved child, that you have been
    deeply hurt.
I feel your pain, and I am confident that God feels it
    as well.

Lift up your tired hands, then, to the Lord!
    Let God strengthen your trembling knees!
      Keep on walking on straight paths,
        so that your limp may not lead
          to a permanent disability.
    God wants you and your grief to be fully healed!

Seek to be at peace with everyone, and seek to live
    a holy life!
Remember that Jesus said:
    How blessed are those who are pure in heart!
      They will see God!

Guard against letting your grief turn you back
    from the grace of God.
I don't want anyone to become like a bitter plant
    that grows up and causes even more troubles
      with its poison.

Be careful also that none of you falls into impurity
   or loses your reverence for God
      and those things God values.

In the strong hands of God,
   all created things will be shaken and removed,
so that those things that cannot be shaken will remain.

Even in our trauma, let us be thankful, then.
   God has made us a part of the kingdom
      that cannot be shaken.

And, thus, let us offer to God acceptable worship
   with reverence and awe!

For our God is a consuming fire who can use our pain
   to burn away dross and uncover that which is pure
      beneath it!

Ephesians 1:16–23
Paraphrased with a focus on human struggle, grief, and pain

I have not stopped giving thanks to God for you. I have heard of your crisis; I have heard of your faith. I am remembering you constantly in my prayers, and this is what I pray:

> I keep asking the God of our Lord, Jesus the Christ, the glorious Father, to give you the gift of the ever-present awareness of God's Spirit.
>
> God's Spirit will give you the wisdom you need, and will also reveal God to you that you may genuinely know God himself, as well as God's immense compassion and power.
>
> I ask that your mind may be continually enlightened to see the light of God shining into your struggle, so that you may know deep in your heart God's hope in and for you now.
>
> I also pray that you may discover how rich are the blessings God promises his people as you walk on through your deep and lonely darkness.
>
> I pray that you may know how very great is God's power constantly at work in those of us who believe.

This power working in us is the same identical power as the mighty strength that God used when he raised Christ from death and seated him at God's right side.

It is the same power that moves mountains, climbs mountains, and cradles us in the Father's hand—so that no possible earthly power can disrupt the touch we have with God, nor the well-being that gives us.

It is the same power that enables God to put all things under the sway of Christ, and that gave Christ to the church as Lord of all things—including tragedy!

This church is the body of Christ, doing Christ's work in the earth. This church is the completion of Christ's work.

It brings to completion the well-being God wants you and all the world to have. I pray God's power for you now!

1 Corinthians 15:51–58
A paraphrase with reference to grief work

Listen, and I will tell you about a mystery.
We shall not all die! But we shall all be changed—
   in a moment,
      in the twinkling of an eye,
         at the last trumpet.
For the trumpet will sound, and the dead will be
   raised beyond the reach of corruption.
And we will be utterly transformed
   (like a caterpillar into a butterfly)!

For this perishable nature of ours must be absorbed by
   imperishability!
These bodies that are mortal must be wrapped in
   immortality!
So—when the perishable puts on the imperishable,
   and the mortal puts on the immortal,
you will realize the truth of this old saying:

   Death is completely swallowed up in victory!
   O Death, where is the triumph you hoped to win?
   O Grave, where is your power to sting us?

It is sin that gives death its power.
It is the law that gives sin its strength.

All thanks be to God who gives us the victory
 through our Lord, Jesus the Christ!
For he has delivered us from
 the fear of death,
  the power of sin, and
   the condemnation of the law.

Psalm 145:13–19
A paraphrase with reference to grief

Your ability to sustain our lives is eternal, O God!
You are in charge of our well-being forever!

The Lord is faithful to his promises!
 And everything God does is good!

God takes initiative to help those who are in trouble.
God uses his power to lift those who have fallen
 as well as those who are knocked down.

God is near to those who call to him;
 who call to him in sincerity.

God supplies the needs of those who honor him.
 He hears our cries,
  saves us—makes us whole,
   and gives us health!

Some Parting Words of Jesus
Adapted from John 14

Shortly before his own death, Jesus said some crucially important words to his followers. It seems appropriate for us to hear them now.

My parting gift to you is peace—peace such as the world cannot give. Allow God to set your troubled hearts at rest. Let God banish your fears. I do not want you to stay in your distress. I do not want you to be daunted. You have heard me say that I am going away, but I will be coming back to you.

I have said all this while I am with you so that when I am executed, your faith will not be shaken. God is sending you another comforter—another counselor —to stand by you. He will be a friend who will help you draw upon God's strength. This spiritual friend will help you cope with life. He will nurture you, comfort you, and guide you. And, He will be with you forever. He will lead you to recognize and accept what is ultimately real.

Then Jesus said:

I must be going now. I am going to show the world that I love God by doing what God has commanded me to do. Get up now. Let us leave this place.

Psalm 27:1–6, 13–14
A paraphrase with reference to grief

The Lord is my light and my salvation;
    whom shall I fear?
The Lord is the stronghold of my life;
    of whom shall I be afraid?

When evildoers assail me, uttering slanders against me,
    my adversaries and foes, they shall stumble and fall.

Though a host encamp against me,
    my heart shall not fear;
though a whole army arise against me,
    yet will I be confident.

One thing have I asked from the Lord,
    that will I seek after;
    that I may dwell in the house of the Lord
        all the days of my life,
    to behold the beauty of the Lord
        and to inquire in his temple.

For God will hide me in his shelter
    in the day of trouble;
God will conceal me under the cover of his tent;
    He will set me high upon a rock.

And now my head shall be lifted up
    above my enemies round about me;
and I will offer in his sanctuary sacrifices
    with shouts of joy.
I will sing and make melody to the Lord. . . .

I believe that I shall see the goodness of the Lord
    in the land of the living!
Wait for the Lord; be strong,
    and let your heart take courage;
Yea, wait for the Lord!

Revelation 7:13–17, 11–12
A paraphrase relating to grief and tribulation

As we stood around that great white throne of God, one of the elders said to me, "Who are these people who are arrayed in white robes? From whence do they come?"

And I said to him, "Lord, only thou knowest."

God said, "Yes! I know them. These are my children who have come out of great tribulation. Now they have washed their robes, and they have become clean in the blood of the Lamb."

Therefore, they are now before the throne of God. They serve him continuously in his temple. He who sits upon the throne shall dwell with them.

Because of him they shall hunger no more, neither shall they thirst; the sun will burn them no longer, nor will any heat they have formerly experienced.

For the Lamb that is in the midst of the throne will keep on feeding them. He shall care for their every need. He shall lead them unto the fountains of refreshing waters; and God himself shall wipe away every tear from their eyes.

All the people stood around the throne and kept on worshiping God. They kept saying: "Amen! Blessing! and Glory! and Wisdom! and Honor! and Power! and Might! be unto our God forever and ever!"

Psalm 85
Paraphrased for someone in grief

I ask you, O God, to make me well and strong again, and I, your chosen child, in whom you have great delight, will then be able to praise and serve you.

I can't let go of my grief without trusting in your constant love, O God. I've got to have your saving help.

I'm now willing to listen to what you're saying to me. I'm willing to act on my response.

You have promised me genuine peace if I do not keep going back to my foolish, destructive ways.

My grief seems more comfortable and less scary than the healthy new ways you offer me. But letting go seems so painful.

I can count on the fact that you, O God, whose personal name is Yahweh, are ready to give me genuine joy and well-being.

Yet, I know that even you, O God, cannot do this if I will not cooperate by trusting Yahweh alone for my health and new life as well as making the choice to go on living. Yahweh will give me the gift of well-being, or, in other words, God's saving presence.

Yahweh promises me that God's own self will be here for me, and that you will be absolutely trustworthy.

Yahweh has assured me "I will remain in the world. I will remain in a seeking, caring, comforting, challenging posture toward you, my child."

But I also know that even God's gift is absolutely useless, and has no ability to make me well and strong apart from my own willingness to respond with action to a personal relationship with God who gives this gift. When I do respond in my thoughts, feelings, and actions—in my mind, heart, and strength—with repentance and faith, then God's love and my faithfulness truly meet.

Meditation on Psalm 85

Psalm 85 is a dramatically significant passage of scripture. As I have faced losses that left me in devastation and terror, I have turned to its pages and heard a word from God that sounds like this.

When I have lost something or someone and am inundated by the ravages of grief, I must respond to the God who created me, redeemed me, and accompanies me in my grief by repentance. Repentance—in the language I grew up with—means remorse, feeling guilty, being sorry about something. In biblical language, repentance means to TURN. It is a navigational term that means to turn toward God, to turn away from myself and from my loss. I have discovered that after an appropriate time of grief work, such a turn becomes possible.

I have learned that when I respond with this "turning kind of repentance," I can turn away from my loss, turn away from my love of my grief, from my fear of the future—and actually turn toward God. Turning toward God is like turning toward the hug the prodigal son received when he returned from the far country into the waiting arms of the father. When I turn toward God, I turn toward the gift of new life and new joy as the son returning home did. I am included in a new partnership after a devastating experience.

Such turning is done through faith. The courage of faith that trusts God alone for my well-being enables God to do for me what I would not allow God to do before faith and repentance were exercised. I receive God's grace through exercising my faith. Such faith is a verb, not a noun.

The psalmist says that when such faith is acted out in repentance "God's love and my faithfulness truly meet, righteousness and peace will embrace" (Ps 85:10). When such a rendezvous happens with God, who shares my deepest grief, resurrection and renewal happen.

My human loyalty will reach up in the response of trust from the earth; God's ability to make me whole, new, and at peace gently descends upon me and into me as a gift from above. Yahweh gives me true well-being as a gift. I welcome the wholeness God offers, and the gift is consummated.

Yahweh causes my personality and my vocation of being God's partner to prosper with the richness of a bounteous harvest. My new-found relationship with Yahweh provides a path for God to enter my personality on a continuing basis. Yahweh and I become companions, friends, and partners in living. God is not just someone I believe in. God becomes someone with whom I share the journey of life.

Furthermore, my new-found strength enables me to relate to others, share our common griefs, and be on vocation with Yahweh—whatever my "job" is, however I earn my paycheck. My joy in life takes the shape of sharing the grace with others that God has given me. Receiving God's grace enables me to be gracious to others.

At the deepest level, to say goodbye to grief is to say hello to God. To say goodbye to grief is to experience a new and deeper relationship with God, who becomes your personal friend as well as your lord and leader.

To know that God loves me and will not allow anything—anything at all—to separate me from God is to know the only truly constant reality in life (see Rom 8:37-39). Faith, hope, and love abide! The greatest of these is love! (1 Cor 13:13.)

Conclusion

After reading these paraphrases, I suggest that you read them in your favorite translation of the Bible. Read them in *Today's English Version,* usually called the Good News translation. Read them in the *New Revised Standard Version.* Read the New Testament passsages in Eugene Peterson's recent paraphrase, *The Message.* Read and re-read these passages and *listen* for a word from God.

These passages offer real hope and genuine help for someone who is at the point of being ready to say goodbye to grief of long standing. I recognize that this is a difficult area to discuss helpfully because people in the grief process are in so many different places in their own journeys—so many different places of readiness either to grieve or to let go of grief.

What I am saying is designed to be helpful to someone who is at the point of staying too long with grief and at the point of being ready to move past grief into the reestablishment of life. I am very aware that some of you may not be at that point, as I have learned with my own griefs as well as with those of people whom I have sought to help as a grief counselor. One *cannot* rush or take short-cuts to the point at which it becomes possible, appropriate, and necessary to say goodbye to grief.

Take your time, but do not think time will cure grief in and of itself. Embrace your pain rather than avoid it. Express your feelings rather than hide them. Remember:

> You're blessed when you feel you've lost what is most dear to you.
> Only then can you be embraced by the One most dear to you.[1]

Note

[1]Matthew 5:4, Eugene Peterson, *The Message* (Colorado Springs CO: NavPress, 1993) 15-16.

Appendix

Helps in Doing Grief Work

Things We Need to Know about Grief

It Is Normal and O.K.:

(1) To feel like crying and to cry
(2) To be angry and feel lots of hostility
—in general, at God, or at the deceased
(3) To feel guilt and/or regretful
—be sure and distinguish between guilt
and false guilt
(4) To want to give up
(5) To be dependent
—appropriate dependence is a strength just as
inappropriate independence is a weakness
(6) To be weak, to need help
(7) To continue some grieving after a long time
(8) To say goodbye at some point
—to your loss,
—to your grief about your loss
(9) To reestablish and go on with your life
(10) To return to happiness as your basic way
of being

It Is Not Generally O.K., Positive, or Healthy:

   (1) To try to be or seem to be too strong

   (2) To try to avoid reality
      —with isolation, activity, drugs, alcohol, eating, etc.

   (3) To try to shield or protect each other from pain

   (4) To drop out of your community of faith

   (5) To see God as being aloof from your pain and struggle

   (6) To try to change too much about your life too quickly

   (7) To try to get over your grief too quickly

   (8) To return to normal activity too soon

   (9) To postpone emotions that come unbidden

  (10) To isolate children from the family experience of loss and grief
      —keep the children with the family as much as possible

  (11) To continue grief indefinitely

Things I Wish People Would Not Say in Times of Grief

(1) "This is the will of God."

(2) "This is punishment for your sins."

(3) "God took your mother because . . ."

(4) "God needed another little flower in his garden, so he took your child."

(5) "There must be a reason we don't understand."

(6) "Time will heal your wounds."

(7) "Just stay busy, that's all you need."

(8) "Don't cry."
"Don't let the children see you cry."
"We've got to be strong to protect Momma."

(9) "Now you're the man of the house."
"Now you've got to be the mommy here."

(10) "You mustn't feel that way."
   "Don't be mad at God."
   "It doesn't make sense to be mad at ____."
   "You shouldn't feel guilty."

(11) "Here, take this sedative. You'll feel better."

(12) "I once knew a person who had exactly
   the same thing happen."
   "One time I had the same experience."

(13) "You'll get to feeling better soon."

(14) "Just pray about it and read your Bible.
   It'll get better."

(15) "We'll get you another doggie."

Jehovah Speaks of Life
by Hardy Clemons

Poets speak of trees that fall,
    Broad and straight and high—
Leaving gaps of emptiness,
    Leaving slots of loneliness,
        Leaving a mute evidence
That we all must die.

Poets speak of muffled oars
    Stealing through the deep—
Seeking heaven, a higher home,
    Seeking rest and joy and peace,
        Saying quietly in the gloom
That death is but sleep.

God speaks not as do the poets
    Jehovah speaks of life!
Life that lives beyond the grave,
    Life in God that will not die,
        Life victorious, transformed,
Eternally endowed!

For Adam's breath is born of God.
    God made us; and God makes
Life to spring within our breasts,
    Life to flame as in response,

Life that lives, though all else dies,
Triumphant in God's power!

The life of our beloved one
   Is not a fallen tree.
Born of God; thrice born is she.
   She is not dead.
      She does not sleep.
         She has not gone away.
She lives! Eternally in God!
   She rises powerful o'er the tomb!
   She shares God's life today!

There She Goes/Here She Comes
by Henry Van Dyke

I am standing on the seashore.
A ship at my side spreads her white sails
    and starts for the blue ocean.

She is an object of beauty and strength.
I stand and watch her until at length.
    She hangs like a speck of white cloud just
    where the sea and sky come down
    and mingle with each other.

Then someone at my side says:
"There she goes."

Gone where?
Gone from my sight—that is all!

She is just as large in mast and hull and spar
As she was when she left my side.

She is just as able to bear her load of living freight
    to the place of destination.
Her diminished size is in me, not in her.

And, just at the moment when someone at my side
    says:

"There, she's gone."
There are other eyes watching her coming
And other voices ready to take up the glad shout:
"Here she comes!"

And, that is dying.